2015

28.50

781.66
ANN

38106000007974

DATE DUE

THE STORY OF

POP HISTORIES

PUNK AND INDIE

MATT ANNISS

A+

Smart Apple Media

Published in the United States by Smart Apple Media
PO Box 3263, Mankato, Minnesota 56002

Copyright © 2014 Arcturus Publishing Limited

The right of Matt Anniss to be identified as the author of this work has been asserted by him in accordance with the Copyright, Designs and Patents Act 1988.

Text: Matt Anniss
Editors: Joe Harris and Rachel Blount
Design: Paul Myerscough and Keith Williams

Picture credits:
Corbis: Roberta Bayley 8, Bettmann 4, Bureau L.A. Collection/Sygma 13, Chris Carroll 14, Kevin P. Casey 19b, Mike Laye 7t, Gary Leonard 11c, Hiroyuki Matsumoto/Amana Images 5, Michael Ochs Archives 10; Shutterstock: Mohammad Fariz Abdullah 24, Christian Bertrand 21bl, S Bukley 19t, Debu55y 16t, Rob van Esch 18t, Featureflash 23t, Andreas Gradin 31, Mat Hayward 22t, Jaguar PS 29b, Aija Lehtonen 22b, 23b, Northfoto 1, 7b, 25b, 29t, Amra Pasic 20t, Mathias Rosenthal 9bl, Nikola Spasenoski 21br, 27b, Ferenc Szelepcsenyi 15t, Debby Wong 26; Wikipedia: Alfio66 17t, Katherine Barton 9br, The Dutch National Archives 6, Pedro Figueiredo 12b, Mike Higgott 11t, Kennysun 28, Livepict.com 17b, Lola's Big Adventure! 20b, Yves Lorson 15b, Me677 9t, Morven 12t, Stig Nygaard 16b, Sceptre 27t, Fabio Venni 25t, Xrayspx 18b.
Cover images: guitarristasmejoresdelmundo.blogspot.co.uk top far right; Shutterstock: Aija Lehtonen top center left, Northfoto top center right, Amra Pasic top left, Mathias Rosenthal main; Wikipedia: momento mori top far left, Helge Øverås top right.

Library of Congress Cataloging-in-Publication Data

Anniss, Matt.
  The story of punk and indie / Matt Anniss.
     pages cm. -- (Pop histories)
  Includes index.
 Summary: "Describes the beginnings and evolution of punk and indie music, spotlighting important artists and songs"--Provided by publisher.
  ISBN 978-1-59920-968-5 (library binding)
 1. Punk rock music--History and criticism--Juvenile literature. 2. Alternative rock music--History and criticism--Juvenile literature. I. Title.
  ML3534.A546 2014
  781.66--dc23
                                2013003611

Printed in China

SL002672US

Supplier 03, Date 0513, Print Run 2376

CONTENTS

Downtown Revolution 4

Anarchy in the UK 6

Do It Yourself 8

Post-Punk 10

Indie-Pop and Gothic Rock 12

The Birth of
Alternative Rock 14

Start the Dance 16

Alternative Goes
Mainstream 18

The Birth of Britpop 20

Stadium Punk 22

What Goes Around,
Comes Around 24

When I Ruled the World 26

Evolving Sounds 28

Glossary 30

Further Information 31

Index 32

DOWNTOWN REVOLUTION

Both punk and indie are styles of music that define themselves against the mainstream. From the start, their histories have been intertwined. The roots of both styles can be traced back to two American rock bands of the late 1960s, MC5 and the Stooges.

Kick Out the Jams

MC5 and the Stooges made rough, raw, angry rock music, the likes of which had never been heard before. When they released their most important records in 1969, there was nothing else around like this. They smashed up their instruments during concerts and made a racket.

New York Noise

The angry antics of MC5 and the Stooges didn't go unnoticed. In New York, a heavy underground rock scene began to spring up around a club in Manhattan called CBGB. There, a number of local bands began making loud, brash, and simple rock music.

PROTO-PUNK

At the heart of the New York underground rock scene were revolutionary bands Television and the New York Dolls. They had taken the alternative rock template of the Stooges and made it even more energetic.

BY MIXING ELEMENTS OF BRITISH GLAM ROCK WITH RAW AMERICAN ROCK, THE NEW YORK DOLLS (PICTURED) PAVED THE WAY FOR THE PUNK REVOLUTION SPEARHEADED BY THE RAMONES.

The Ramones built their reputation as the first real punk band thanks to a series of concerts at the legendary CBGB club in New York.

Enter the Ramones

The band that really made the difference was the Ramones. They played their first gig at CBGB in August 1974. By the end of the year, they'd played over 70 shows at the venue and built up a cult following.

Proper Punks

The Ramones were arguably the first real punk band. They weren't trained musicians and tried to make their songs as easy to play as possible. They described their loud, raw sound as "dumb rock and roll music".

Do It Yourself

The Ramones' style of music quickly became known as punk rock. Their 1976 album, *Ramones*, became the blueprint for punk music. Teenagers on both sides of the Atlantic Ocean were inspired to pick up guitars and do it themselves.

PLAYLIST
THE ROOTS OF PUNK

The Sex Pistols—*God Save the Queen* (A & M, 1977)

The Stooges—*No Fun* (Elektra, 1969)

The New York Dolls—*Personality Crisis* (Mercury, 1973)

Patti Smith—*Free Money* (Arista, 1975)

The Ramones—*Blitzkrieg Bop* (Sire, 1979)

ANARCHY IN THE UK

Since the late 1970s, both American and British bands have played a part in developing the sounds of punk and indie. In 1976, the sound of New York bands inspired teenagers in the UK to start writing their own punk rock songs.

London Calling

In 1976, three punk bands emerged from the dirty backstreet clubs of London: the Damned, the Clash, and the Sex Pistols. To begin with, few people took notice. There was one man, though, who believed in their potential.

Meet Malcolm McLaren

That man was Malcolm McLaren, an eccentric businessman turned band manager with a big shock of curly red hair. Under his guidance, the Sex Pistols became the most famous punk band in the world.

IMPORTANT CONCERT

In June 1976, the Sex Pistols played a concert at Manchester's Lesser Free Trade Hall. Although there were just 40 people present, the concert would have a huge impact. After seeing the "gig", audience members went on to form a number of now-legendary bands, including Joy Division and the Smiths.

TEENAGERS WERE DRAWN TO PUNK NOT JUST BECAUSE OF THE LOUD NATURE OF THE MUSIC, BUT ALSO THE ANGRY ATTITUDE OF BANDS SUCH AS THE SEX PISTOLS (PICTURED).

Bad Attitude

The Sex Pistols' music was extreme even by punk standards, but it was more their attitude that attracted fans. Teenagers loved the fact that they smashed things up and criticized people in authority, such as politicians and the British royal family.

SWEAR ON AIR

In 1977, the Sex Pistols made the front page of newspapers in the UK after swearing in a live TV interview. It was the first time anyone had sworn on British TV, and there was outrage in the press. Suddenly, punk was big news.

The Birth of "Indie"

The Sex Pistols broke up in 1978, but by then, punk had changed the music industry. Thousands of teenagers around the UK had been inspired to form their own bands, put on concerts, or start record labels. The independent music revolution had begun.

LIVING LEGEND

JOHN LYDON

John Lydon rose to fame as the lead singer of the Sex Pistols. With his ripped clothes, wild hair, and aggressive attitude, Lydon was the stereotypical punk rocker. Although the Sex Pistols split up in 1978, he is still a prominent musician and celebrity worldwide.

DO IT YOURSELF

The impact that punk made in the 1970s went far beyond introducing the world to a loud new form of rock music. Its independent ethos inspired a whole generation of teenagers to take music and fashion into their own hands.

Angry Reaction

Some people argue that the punk movement was a reaction against 1970s pop music. They say that teenagers were bored of progressive rock, disco and glam rock, and rebelled against them by creating noisy, cutting-edge music.

Accessible Music

Others disagree with this argument, saying that punk was attractive to teenagers because it was accessible to all. It didn't matter if you had no musical training – you could just pick up a guitar and play.

MASSIVE IMPACT

Whatever the reason for punk's runaway success, it had a huge impact on how teenagers thought about music, fashion and art. Many thought that if they could make music with little or no training, they could do other things, too.

Get On with It

Soon, a "do-it-yourself" attitude began to thrive within the punk scene. Some people were inspired to create their own homemade magazines, known as "fanzines", while others tried their hand at making outrageous clothes.

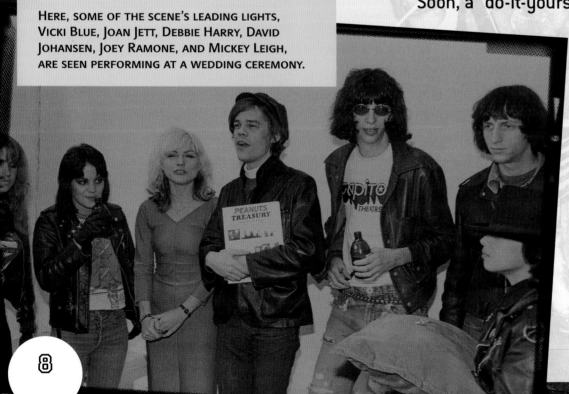

HERE, SOME OF THE SCENE'S LEADING LIGHTS, VICKI BLUE, JOAN JETT, DEBBIE HARRY, DAVID JOHANSEN, JOEY RAMONE, AND MICKEY LEIGH, ARE SEEN PERFORMING AT A WEDDING CEREMONY.

STARTING UP

The do-it-yourself attitude of punk also inspired a number of music fans to gatecrash the music industry by starting their own record labels. These are the companies that manufacture and sell music.

THE PUNK LOOK FEATURED BRIGHTLY COLOURED MOHAWK HAIRSTYLES, BODY PIERCINGS, AND OUTRAGEOUS CLOTHES.

Major Movement

Before punk, few had thought about setting up their own record labels. Afterwards, thanks to the success of companies such as Stiff, 4AD, Rough Trade and Factory, independent labels became the backbone of the punk and indie scenes.

The Birth of Indie

The "indie" label that showed the way was Factory. Founded by Tony Wilson in 1978, the Manchester, England-based label proved that you could build a successful business out of releasing interesting, cutting-edge music.

INDIE HERO

MANI on TONY WILSON
[THE STONE ROSES]

"Everyone in the indie world owes a debt of gratitude to Tony. He showed that anyone can start their own thing up. Everyone learned a lot from Factory."

Mani (pictured)

POST-PUNK

By 1978, punk rock was on its last legs. It was less popular, and many of the scene's leading bands were looking at other types of music for inspiration. In its place came a new sound with a new "anything goes" ethos: post-punk.

Oi!

To start with, not everyone was ready to give up on punk. Punk purists continued to play the music, either as part of Britain's "oi" movement or the hardcore punk scene that began to develop in the United States.

Changing Times

These people were in a minority, however. Many "first generation" punk bands began to find the sound too restrictive. They were anxious to make music that took the "anything goes" attitude of punk in new directions.

FIRST ISSUE

Arguably, the first post-punk band to emerge was Public Image Limited. Set up by former Sex Pistols singer John Lydon, Public Image Limited made heavy music influenced by a Jamaican style of music called dub reggae and an experimental style from Germany called "Krautrock".

Second Edition

Punk had been about pushing musical boundaries, but post-punk took it further. Inspired by Public Image Limited's noisy fusions of punk and dub reggae, bands around the world began to take post-punk in many different directions.

DESPITE THEIR NEW YORK POST-PUNK DANCE ROOTS, BLONDIE ENJOYED GREAT SUCCESS IN THE POP CHARTS AROUND THE WORLD.

NEW YORK NOISE

In New York, a "dance-punk" scene began to emerge. There, bands such as ESG, Talking Heads, and Blondie fused punk with sounds borrowed from dance music styles such as disco and electronica.

Northern Uprising

In Northern English cities such as Sheffield and Manchester, bands such as Cabaret Voltaire, Joy Division, and A Certain Ratio mixed gloomy guitars with sounds created using electronic instruments such as synthesizers.

Constant Evolution

As the 1970s turned into the 1980s, post-punk music continued to evolve. Backed by independent labels, it would soon form the basis of what would become known as "indie music".

PLAYLIST
POST-PUNK

Public Image Limited —*Public Image* (Virgin, 1978)

Talking Heads—*Burning Down the House* (Sire, 1983)

Blondie—*House of Glass* (Capitol, 1979)

The Pop Group—*She's Beyond Good and Evil* (Radar Records, 1979)

A Certain Ratio—*All Night Party* (Factory Records, 1980)

INDIE-POP AND GOTHIC ROCK

In the early 1980s, the indie music scene was in good health, particularly in the United Kingdom. While American teenagers were lapping up new rock styles such as heavy metal, bands in the UK continued to create new styles of indie music.

Proto-Goth

One of the key developments was a sound called "gothic rock", or "goth". It had originally emerged around 1979, when journalists first used the term to describe the music of some post-punk bands.

SINGER DINAH CANCER WAS THE DRIVING FORCE BEHIND 45 GRAVE, ONE OF AMERICA'S FIRST GOTHIC ROCK BANDS.

GOTHIC ROCK

The beginning of a distinct goth sound can be traced back to a 1979 song called *Bela Lugosi's Dead* by Bauhaus. Written as a tribute to an actor famous for his roles in horror films, it was dark and incredibly atmospheric.

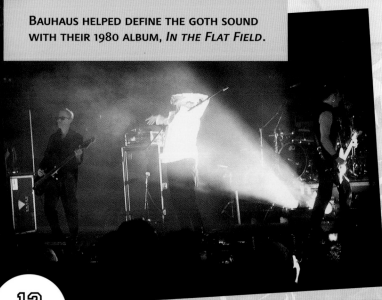

BAUHAUS HELPED DEFINE THE GOTH SOUND WITH THEIR 1980 ALBUM, *IN THE FLAT FIELD*.

Dark Days

Where Bauhaus led, others followed. Thanks to the success of groups such as the Cure and the Sisters of Mercy, goth became a full-fledged style of indie music. It also influenced U.S. bands 45 Grave and Christian Death to create their own fusion of punk and goth, called "deathrock".

Upbeat Alternative

Goth wasn't the only style of indie music to emerge from the post-punk scene. Slowly, a sound was developing that would become known as indie-pop. Influenced by 1960s pop music as well as post-punk, indie-pop was more upbeat than goth.

Indie Heroes

The band that really put indie-pop on the map was the Smiths. Founded in Manchester in 1982, they wrote songs that combined moody lyrics with bright guitar riffs. By the mid 1980s, the Smiths were the most popular indie band in the UK and had built up a cult following in the United States.

Pop Heroes

Unlike the deliberately difficult punk bands, indie-pop acts made music that sounded good on the radio. By the end of the 1980s, some indie-pop bands were almost as popular as mainstream rock groups.

INSIDE THE SOUND

GOTHIC ROCK

Gothic rock music was so called because it was deliberately dark and moody. Many goth bands gained inspiration from horror books or films, such as *Dracula* or *Frankenstein*. The songs written by goth bands often dealt with dark subjects, such as death and obsessive love.

THE BIRTH OF ALTERNATIVE ROCK

During the 1980s, life could be hard for American bands playing indie music. The scene was relatively small and kept alive by the enthusiasm of a handful of concert promoters, bands, and label owners.

SONIC YOUTH WOULD LATER GO ON TO BE INTERNATIONAL ALTERNATIVE ROCK STARS, BUT DURING THE 1980S, THEY WERE STUCK ON THE AMERICAN COLLEGE ROCK CIRCUIT.

American Rock

During the 1980s, the American music scene was dominated by mainstream rock, heavy metal, rap, and pop. Bands who had been inspired by the post-punk movement to make alternative rock music were largely overlooked.

AMERICAN INDIE

There were many independent record labels in the United States pushing underground rock music in the years following post-punk. However, they found it hard to get their records played on radio stations.

Radio Stars

The savior of American indie music was college radio. College radio stations were run by and for university students. They were often very supportive of little-known American indie bands.

Alternative Boom

The name change came at a good time for American indie music. Many of the scene's best bands, such as REM, the Pixies, and Jane's Addiction, were becoming well-known outside of the alternative scene.

On the Verge of Greatness

By the tail end of the decade, American alternative rock was becoming big business. Soon, a new style would emerge from the city of Seattle that would take the music worldwide. Alternative rock was on the verge of going mainstream.

College Rock

As a result, a college rock scene developed. It was musically diverse, containing everything from the post-punk noise of Sonic Youth and indie-pop of REM, to the punk-influenced sounds of Husker Du and Nine Inch Nails.

Alternative Rock

Initially, college rock bands received little attention outside the college radio scene. However, as the 1980s wore on, the scene began to spread beyond college campuses. As it grew in popularity, it was renamed "alternative rock".

LIVING LEGENDS

REM

REM was formed in Athens, Georgia, in 1980, by a group of students who shared a love of New York punk. After dropping out of college, they drove between concert venues in a small van and lived on two dollars a day each. Eventually, they became one of the most popular alternative rock bands on the planet.

START THE DANCE

While alternative rock was on the verge of a major breakthrough in America, indie music in the UK was undergoing its own major upheaval. As the 1980s came to a close, indie-pop was turning into indie-dance.

Seeds of Change

Ever since the post-punk days of the early 1980s, some indie bands had included dance music elements in their songs. Yet until 1989, they were a relative rarity. Jangly indie-pop and moody goth songs were much more popular.

HAVING PLAYED AN IMPORTANT ROLE IN THE DEVELOPMENT OF INDIE DURING THE EARLY 1980S, MANCHESTER BANDS SPEARHEADED THE INDIE-DANCE REVOLUTION OF THE 1980S AND '90S.

Dance Music Revolution

In 1989, the UK was enjoying a love affair with dance music. The arrival of house music boosted attendances at nightclubs. Indie musicians found themselves dancing in dark cellars to the latest dance sounds.

THE HAPPY MONDAYS WERE ONE OF THE FIRST BANDS TO SUCCESSFULLY COMBINE INDIE-ROCK GUITARS AND MODERN DANCE BEATS.

Indie Embraces Dance

Given this huge change, it was almost inevitable that some indie bands would embrace dance music and club culture. Manchester's Factory Records, whose founders also owned a nightclub called the Hacienda, was naturally at the forefront.

From the Factory Floor

Factory bands the Happy Mondays and New Order led the way, releasing records that fused indie-pop and dance beats. Fellow Manchester band the Stone Roses were also hugely popular. They mixed indie-rock with loose funk grooves and hip-hop beats.

Changing Times

Primal Scream had been one of the pioneers of the "indie-pop" sound of the mid 1980s. They fell in love with the dance music culture, and in 1990, they recorded one of the defining indie-dance albums of all time, *Screamadelica*.

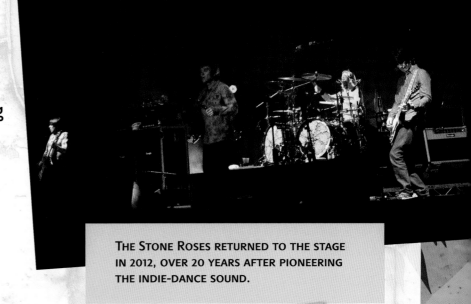

THE STONE ROSES RETURNED TO THE STAGE IN 2012, OVER 20 YEARS AFTER PIONEERING THE INDIE-DANCE SOUND.

LASTING LEGACY

The indie-dance movement of 1989–1991 had a lasting effect on indie music. Although it went out of fashion, since the 2000s, a new generation of indie-dance, or alternative dance bands, has emerged in America and the UK. These owe a lot to indie-dance pioneers of the 1980s and '90s.

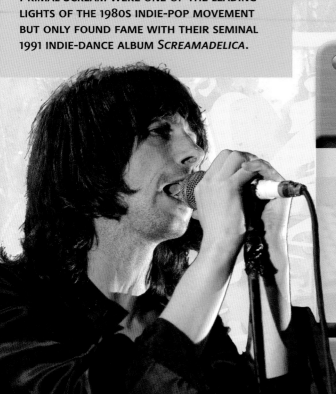

PRIMAL SCREAM WERE ONE OF THE LEADING LIGHTS OF THE 1980S INDIE-POP MOVEMENT BUT ONLY FOUND FAME WITH THEIR SEMINAL 1991 INDIE-DANCE ALBUM *SCREAMADELICA*.

● PLAYLIST

INDIE-DANCE

New Order—*Round and Round* (Factory, 1989)

Happy Mondays—*Hallelujah* (Factory, 1989)

The Stone Roses—*Fools Gold* (Silvertone, 1989)

Primal Scream – *Loaded* (Creation, 1990)

The Farm—*Groovy Train* (Produce, 1990)

Lovekittens – *What Goes On* (Sheer Joy, 1991)

ALTERNATIVE GOES MAINSTREAM

In the city of Seattle, an alternative rock revolution was brewing. Between 1989 and 1990, a number of the city's bands rose to prominence playing a tough new style of indie music: grunge.

Grunge Sound

Grunge was different from other styles of alternative rock. Sludgy, fuzzy, and distorted, it took more influences from American hardcore punk than British indie-pop. The musicians who made it dressed scruffily, choosing to shun fashion in favor of clothes bought at thrift stores.

THE CITY OF SEATTLE WAS THE UNLIKELY BIRTHPLACE OF GRUNGE, THE STYLE THAT WOULD TAKE ALTERNATIVE ROCK TO THE TOP OF THE CHARTS.

Sub Pop

The independent record label behind the grunge sound was a Seattle-based company called Sub Pop. During the late 1980s, it released a number of influential albums by pioneering grunge bands such as Mudhoney and Soundgarden.

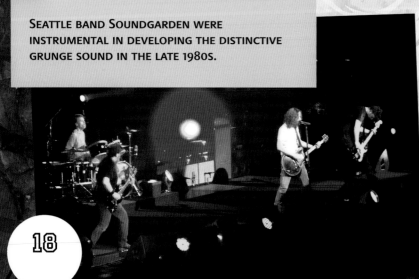

SEATTLE BAND SOUNDGARDEN WERE INSTRUMENTAL IN DEVELOPING THE DISTINCTIVE GRUNGE SOUND IN THE LATE 1980S.

Mixed Reaction

To begin with, reaction to grunge from music fans was mixed. Some within the alternative rock and indie scenes were enthusiastic, but for the first few years, it was largely ignored.

Major Label Interest

The major labels were paying attention, though. In 1990, Seattle bands Soundgarden, Alice In Chains, and Nirvana all signed big-money contracts with major record labels. It was only a matter of time before records by grunge artists stormed the music charts.

BONO ON KURT COBAIN
[U2]

"I remember watching Kurt come through and thinking 'this music is nuclear.' Nirvana raised the temperature. They made everything else look silly."

Bono (pictured)

Surprise Hit

In 1991, Nirvana released an album called *Nevermind*. Packed with strong grunge songs, it proved hugely popular. By December 1991, it was selling 40,000 copies a week. By January 1992, it had hit the top of the U.S. album charts.

Unlikely Heroes

Nirvana were unlikely superstars. Their front man, Kurt Cobain, had major problems with depression and drug addiction. He didn't particularly enjoy the fame the band's success brought and killed himself in 1994, at 27 years old.

NIRVANA FRONTMAN KURT COBAIN WAS ONE OF THE BIGGEST STARS OF ALTERNATIVE ROCK.

IMPORTANT ALBUM

The success of *Nevermind* proved that albums by alternative rock bands could sell in big numbers. Over the next few years, many alternative rock bands became international superstars. Alternative rock was now mainstream rock.

THE BIRTH OF BRITPOP

By the middle of the 1990s, alternative rock and indie music were more popular than ever before. Once again, the style was changing. While American alternative rock continued to be popular, British indie music hit back.

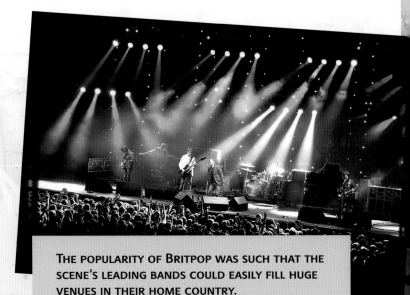

THE POPULARITY OF BRITPOP WAS SUCH THAT THE SCENE'S LEADING BANDS COULD EASILY FILL HUGE VENUES IN THEIR HOME COUNTRY.

Hard Work

In the early 1990s, British indie bands found it hard to make much of an impact around the world because of the popularity of grunge bands such as Nirvana and Pearl Jam. But by 1993, all that was beginning to change.

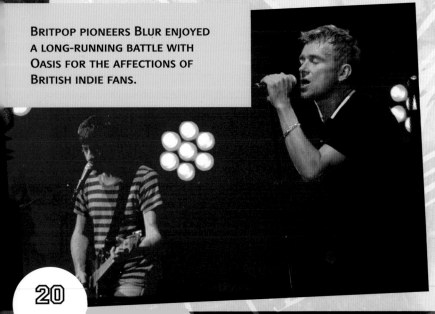

BRITPOP PIONEERS BLUR ENJOYED A LONG-RUNNING BATTLE WITH OASIS FOR THE AFFECTIONS OF BRITISH INDIE FANS.

British Sound

In a bid to distance themselves from American alternative rock bands, a number of indie groups from the UK began to make music that was distinctly British. Instead of mimicking grunge, they wrote fun songs that mocked aspects of British life.

Modern Life Is Rubbish

In the early years, the two prime movers behind this new "Britpop" style were London-based bands Blur and Suede. Blur defined the Britpop sound with their 1994 album *Parklife*. It was a roaring success in the UK.

Bitter Rivalry

By the end of 1994, Blur had a serious rival for the crown of "top British band". Oasis, from Manchester, pushed a more rock-influenced take on the Britpop sound. They became big stars following the release of their first album, *Definitely Maybe*.

The Battle of Britpop

Blur and Oasis became big rivals. In 1995, they both released songs on the same day to see who would reach number one in the British pop charts. The press called it "The Battle of Britpop".

Huge Success

The Battle of Britpop helped raise the profile of British indie music worldwide. Soon, other Britpop bands such as Pulp, Suede, and Supergrass were enjoying great success.

INSIDE THE SOUND

BRITPOP

Britpop differed from alternative rock and grunge in a number of ways. Many Britpop songs were written to sound a little like classic British pop and rock records from the 1960s. The Beatles, in particular, were a huge influence.

GOLDEN ERA

Britpop was a golden period for British indie music. In the UK, many of the scene's top bands became superstars. However, in the United States, their success was limited.

BEFORE HE BECAME THE "GODFATHER OF BRITPOP", OASIS'S NOEL GALLAGHER WORKED BACKSTAGE AT CONCERTS BY MANCHESTER BAND INSPIRAL CARPETS.

ALTHOUGH PULP BECAME POPULAR DURING THE BRITPOP ERA, FRONTMAN JARVIS COCKER (PICTURED) ACTUALLY FORMED THE BAND IN 1979.

STADIUM PUNK

Punk didn't wither and die in the post-punk years. In fact, it retained a core fan base, particularly in the United States, and continued to evolve. By the middle of the 1990s, a major punk revival was underway.

THE POPULARITY OF THE AMERICAN PUNK REVIVAL HAS TURNED BANDS SUCH AS THE DROPKICK MURPHYS (PICTURED) INTO STARS.

Hardcore Uproar

During the 1980s, a distinctive hardcore punk scene took shape in the United States, where bands such as Black Flag and Bad Religion kept the sound alive. It gained little mainstream attention, though the hardcore punk sound influenced some alternative rock and grunge bands.

MOST MODERN PUNK FANS WEREN'T ALIVE WHEN THE SOUND FIRST EMERGED FROM NEW YORK CITY.

PUNK RETURNS

By the mid 1990s, a punk revival was taking shape. This time, though, the sound had fewer rough edges than the original punk sound. For this reason, the sound became known as "pop-punk".

Pop-Punk Pioneers

The leaders of the pop-punk revival were two American bands, Green Day and the Offspring. Having built up a large fan base through their releases on independent labels, both were signed to major labels in the early 1990s.

OK Dookie

The album that signaled pop-punk's acceptance into the mainstream was Green Day's *Dookie*. Released in 1994, it went on to sell over nine million copies in two years.

Record Numbers

By 1998, the Offspring had joined Green Day at the top of the U.S. album charts. The lead single from their *Americana* album, *Pretty Fly (for a White Guy)*, was downloaded 22 million times when it was leaked on the Internet prior to release.

Massive Fan Base

In the years that followed, pop-punk increased in mainstream popularity. Offspring and Green Day continued to lead the way. They were now so popular that they could play concerts in massive stadiums.

Superstars

Since the early 2000s, pop-punk has continued to be hugely popular. Blink 182, Jimmy Eat World, and Fall Out Boy have become global superstars. The era of stadium punk has arrived.

BY PLAYING A POP-PUNK STYLE THAT APPEALS TO TEENAGERS, BLINK 182 HAVE HELPED SAVE PUNK ROCK FROM CERTAIN DEATH.

LIVING LEGENDS

GREEN DAY

Since forming in 1987, Green Day has become the biggest punk band on the planet. Since releasing their number one album *Dookie* in 1993, the band has sold more than 69 million records worldwide. In 2010, they wrote the world's first punk musical, based on their acclaimed 2004 album *American Idiot*.

WHAT COES AROUND, COMES AROUND

The early 2000s was a time of great change in the punk and indie scene. While indie-pop and pop-punk bands continued to be popular with mainstream audiences, many musicians in the underground indie scene began to look to post-punk for inspiration.

MUSICAL CYCLES

Musicians have always looked to the past for inspiration. During the Britpop era, this meant 1960s and 1970s guitar pop. When the 1990s punk revival was taking shape, it was to American hardcore punk that bands looked for inspiration.

1980s Inspiration

During the early 2000s, a number of bands based in the United States and UK began listening to classic post-punk records from the likes of the Clash, Public Image Limited, and ESG.

Post-Punk Revival

To begin with, there were four bands that spearheaded the "post-punk revival". They were Franz Ferdinand from Glasgow, Scotland, Swedish band the Hives, and the White Stripes and the Strokes from the United States.

Big in the UK

All of these bands, even those from the United States, made their name in the UK. This was because mainstream music fans in the UK were often more supportive of indie bands. It wasn't long, though, before American bands found fame back home.

SCOTTISH BAND FRANZ FERDINAND WERE ONE OF THE FIRST BANDS OF THE 2000S TO BASE THEIR STYLE ON EARLY '80S POST-PUNK.

FORMER HUSBAND-AND-WIFE COUPLE MEG AND JACK WHITE, BETTER KNOWN AS THE WHITE STRIPES, BECAME FAMOUS IN THE UK BEFORE MAKING IT BIG IN AMERICA.

PLAYLIST
POST-PUNK REVIVAL

The Strokes—*Hard to Explain* (RCA, 2001)

Kings of Leon—*The Bucket* (RCA, 2004)

LCD Soundsystem—*Losing My Edge* (DFA, 2002)

Franz Ferdinand—*Darts of Pleasure* (Domino, 2003)

The White Stripes—*Seven Nation Army* (XL, 2003)

Arctic Monkeys—*Bet You Look Good on the Dancefloor* (Domino, 2005)

Post-Revival

The scene quickly spiralled. Soon, more bands influenced by post-punk and the proto-punk sounds of MC5 began to record hits. The Killers, Kaiser Chiefs, Kings of Leon, Bloc Party, and the Editors all rose to prominence.

MONKEY MAGIC

Perhaps the most notable band to emerge from the 2000s post-punk scene was the Arctic Monkeys. They rose to fame after being a big hit on social media site Myspace.

SWEDISH BAND THE HIVES PLAYED AN INTEGRAL ROLE IN MAKING THE POST-PUNK REVIVAL OF THE 2000S POPULAR.

Losing My Edge

In New York, an independent record label called DFA built up a considerable following by fusing post-punk rock with dance beats. Label bands the Rapture and LCD Soundsystem led the way, ushering in a new wave of post-punk indie-dance.

25

WHEN I RULED THE WORLD

Since the turn of the century, many bands have emerged from the independent music scene and gone on to become global icons. In the twenty-first century, the mainstream appeal of indie music shows no signs of waning.

Two Sides to Every Story

The first decade of the twenty-first century saw two distinct sounds emerge on either side of the Atlantic, both with roots in the small, independent label scene. In the United States, a sound called "emo" began to take the college rock circuit by storm.

EMOTIONAL PUNK

Emo has its roots in the 1980s hardcore punk scene, but it wasn't until the 2000s that it became hugely popular. Then, fans began to lap up the emotional lyrics and heavy punk guitar riffs of Jimmy Eat World and Dashboard Confessional.

Independent Roots

Meanwhile, another, more radio-friendly version of indie music was taking shape on the other side of the Atlantic. These indie sounds spawned a number of bands that would go on to become huge stars around the world.

Major Act

By far the most famous of these was Coldplay. After starting out releasing music on tiny independent record labels, they became famous around the world following the release of a song called *Yellow* in 2000.

THE VIVA LA VIDA TOUR SAW COLDPLAY
PLAY AT OVER 150 VENUES WORLDWIDE.

Stadium Indie

The brand of indie-rock made famous by bands such as Coldplay, Muse, Modest Mouse, Deathcab For Cutie, and Arcade Fire is perfectly suited to mainstream audiences. All of these bands make music that suits big concert venues and music festivals.

Festival Frenzy

The mainstream success of stadium indie bands has helped fuel a revival in music festivals. Once, music festivals were a celebration of obscure underground music. Now, top festivals pay hundreds of thousands of dollars to secure big-name indie acts such as Coldplay and Arcade Fire.

LIKE MANY STADIUM INDIE BANDS, DEATHCAB FOR CUTIE HAVE MADE THE MOVE FROM UNDERGROUND HEROES TO GLOBAL POP STARS.

MIXED VIEWS

Some fans of underground indie music dislike stadium indie bands. However, these bands have helped turn indie-rock into one of the most popular forms of music on the planet.

HAVING STARTED LIFE PLAYING TINY CONCERT VENUES, ARCADE FIRE CAN NOW FILL HUGE ARENAS FOR THEIR SHOWS.

● PLAYLIST
STADIUM INDIE

The Killers—*Somebody Told Me* (Island/Lizard King, 2004)

Arcade Fire—*Wake Up* (Rough Trade, 2005)

Coldplay—*Viva La Vida* (Parlophone, 2008)

Death Cab for Cutie—*Soul Meets Body* (Atlantic, 2005)

EVOLVING SOUNDS

In the 40 years since punk first emerged from the clubs of New York, the indie music scene has changed beyond all recognition. Now, it's in better health than it has ever been.

Online Revolution

The development of the Internet has been crucial to the spread of indie music. Thanks to video sharing and social media sites such as YouTube, Facebook, and Twitter, as well as music-sharing sites such as SoundCloud and Spotify, bands and labels can now promote their music to millions of people around the world.

Direct Selling

Some bands have even taken to sidestepping independent labels altogether. Web sites such as Bandcamp allow ambitious indie and punk bands to sell their music direct to fans, without the need to sign to a record label.

Free Downloads

Even some well-known bands have tried selling to fans directly. Radiohead, pioneers of "indietronica"– a fusion of indie-rock and electronica—have made a number of their albums available to fans free of charge, via their web site.

THE ARCTIC MONKEYS FAMOUSLY USED INTERNET SOCIAL NETWORKS TO BUILD UP A HUGE FOLLOWING, A MOVE THAT HAS SINCE BEEN COPIED BY MANY INDIE BANDS.

Vibrant Scene

Away from the mainstream, the indie music scene is healthier than it has ever been. Indie labels continue to promote interesting new music, while an increase in enthusiasm for live music has led to soaring numbers at concerts.

New Forms

The music continues to evolve, too. In recent years, indie-dance has made a comeback thanks to the "nu-rave" phenomenon, established acts such as Radiohead have pushed the boundaries by working with electronica producers, and indie folk has begun to gain in popularity

LIVING LEGENDS

RADIOHEAD

Radiohead began life as a traditional indie-rock band and first found worldwide acclaim with their 1993 debut album, *Pablo Honey*. After releasing a successful follow-up, they switched focus and began including more electronic elements in their tracks on 1997's *OK, Computer*. It is still thought of as a classic. Since then, they have continued to be at the forefront of the indietronica scene.

MOVING FORWARD

Wherever you look, indie music is moving forward. Bands continue to emerge from the independent music scene, break through, and then go on to bigger and better things. The indie scene is the breeding ground for next year's rock and pop superstars.

FLORENCE WELCH, SINGER OF FLORENCE AND THE MACHINE, HAS MADE A CAREER OUT OF SONGS THAT MIX INDIE, POP, ROCK, FOLK, AND DANCE MUSIC SOUNDS.

GLOSSARY

alternative Something that's different.

audience The people at a concert.

blueprint A detailed outline or plan of action.

defining Describing something clearly.

diverse A wide range of different things.

electronica Music created using electronic instruments.

emerge To come into existence and develop.

ethos A belief.

evolve To change over time.

experimental Based on new ideas.

fanzine A homemade magazine.

fused Joined together, for instance, when two forms of music are combined.

gig A concert.

independent label A record label that is not owned by a big company and therefore operates independently.

inevitable Bound to happen.

influential Something that inspires people to do something similar.

legendary Something or someone that goes down in history for being of huge importance.

mainstream Popular, known, and liked by a lot of people.

major label A large record label that sells records around the world.

manufacture To make in a factory.

overlooked Ignored.

phenomenon An amazing event or series of events.

pioneers People who are the first to do something.

record label A company that specializes in making and selling music.

restrictive Limiting.

revolutionary Something that changes the course of history.

synthesizer An electronic instrument that is played like a piano.

underground Not widely known or popular with large numbers of people.

upheaval Massive change.

venue A place used to host events or concerts.

FURTHER INFORMATION

Further Reading

Combat Rock: A History of Punk by Lora Greene (CreateSpace, 2012)

The History of Indie-Rock by Jennifer Skancke (Lucent Books, 2007)

Kidz Bop: Be a Pop Star!: Start Your Own Band, Book Your Own Gigs, and Become a Rock and Roll Phenom! by Kimberly Potts (Adams Media, 2011)

Play It Loud!: The Rebellious History of Music by Sara Gilbert (Compass Point Books, 2010)

Web Sites

http://www.allmusic.com/style/grunge-ma0000002626
Check out the new and classic grunge albums, artists, and songs on the excellent All Music web site.

http://www.rollingstone.com/music/lists/the-500-greatest-songs-of-all-time-20110407
The stories behind the 500 greatest rock and pop songs of all time, picked by the leading U.S. music magazine, Rolling Stone.

http://www.spin.com
Spin magazine has been championing punk and alternative music in its many forms since 1985. Read about all the latest news and releases online.

http://www.youtube.com/music/alternative
Watch the latest music videos and classic clips from all the hottest indie and alternative rock bands.

INDEX

A Certain Ratio 11
Alice In Chains 19
alternative rock 4, 14–15, 16, 18, 19, 20, 21, 22
Arcade Fire 27
Arctic Monkeys 25, 28

Bauhaus 12
Blink 182 23
Blur 20, 21
Britpop 20–21, 24

Cabaret Voltaire 11
Clash, the 6, 7, 24
Coldplay 26, 27
college radio 14, 15
college rock 14, 15, 26
Cure, the 12, 13

Damned, the 6

emo 26
ESG 11, 24

Factory Records 9, 11, 16
Franz Ferdinand 24, 25

goth 12, 13, 16
gothic rock 12, 13
Green Day 22, 23
grunge 18–19, 20, 21, 22

independent label 9, 11, 14, 18, 22, 25, 26, 28
indie-dance 16–17, 25, 29
indie-pop 12–13, 15, 16, 17, 18, 24
indie-rock 16, 17, 27, 28, 29
indietronica 28, 29

Jimmy Eat World 23, 26
Joy Division 6, 11

Killers, the 25, 27

London 6, 7, 20
Lydon, John 7, 10, 11

major labels 19, 22
Manchester 6, 9, 11, 13, 16, 17, 21
MC5 4, 5, 25
McLaren, Malcolm 6
Muse 27

New Order 17
New York 4, 5, 6, 10, 11, 15, 22, 25, 28
New York Dolls, the 4, 5
Nirvana 19, 20

Oasis 20, 21
Offspring, the 22, 23

Pearl Jam 20
Primal Scream 17
Public Image Limited 10, 11, 24
Pulp 21
punk
  hardcore punk 10, 18, 22, 24, 26
  pop-punk 22, 23, 24
  post-punk 10–11, 12, 13, 14, 15, 16, 22, 24, 25
  post-punk revival 24, 25
  punk revival 22, 24

Radiohead 28, 29
Ramones, the 4, 5
REM 15

Seattle 15, 18, 19
Sex Pistols, the 6, 7, 10
Sheffield 11
Smiths, the 6, 13
Soundgarden 18, 19
Stone Roses, the 9, 17
Stooges, the 4, 5
Strokes, the 24, 25
Suede 20, 21

White Stripes, the 24, 25